Introduction :

In the digital age, making money online has become more accessible than ever before. With the right strategies, tools, and mindset, anyone can start generating income through the power of the internet. Whether you're looking to supplement your existing income, start a side hustle, or build a full-time business, the opportunities are endless.

However, with so many different methods, platforms, and tools available, it can be difficult to know where to start. That's why we've created "The Ultimate Guide to Making Money Online", a comprehensive resource designed to help you navigate the world of online income and achieve your financial goals.

This guide will cover everything you need to know about making money online, from the foundational principles and strategies, to the specific tactics and tools that can help you generate income. We'll cover topics like identifying your niche, building your online presence, creating valuable content, and monetizing your efforts through advertising, affiliate marketing, sponsored content, and more.

Whether you're a complete beginner or an experienced online entrepreneur, this guide is designed to help you take your income generation to the next level. We'll provide practical tips, real-world examples, and actionable steps you can take to start making money online today.

So if you're ready to harness the power of the internet and start generating income on your own terms, let's dive in and get started!

The internet has opened up a world of opportunities for anyone looking to make money online. From selling products and services, to monetizing content through ads or sponsorships, to participating in the sharing economy, there are countless ways to generate income through digital channels. And with the global pandemic driving even more business and communication online, the potential for making money through the internet has only increased.

However, with this wealth of opportunities comes a new set of challenges. With so many different ways to make money online, it can be difficult to know which strategies are most effective, how to stand out in a crowded marketplace, and how to avoid scams or pitfalls that can waste your time and resources.

That's why "The Ultimate Guide to Making Money Online" is such a valuable resource. By providing a comprehensive overview of the key principles, strategies, and tools for making money online, this guide will help you cut through the noise and focus on the most important aspects of building a successful online income stream.

Whether you're interested in starting a blog, creating a YouTube channel, selling products on Etsy or Amazon, or pursuing any other online income opportunity, this guide will provide you with the knowledge and skills you need to succeed. We'll cover everything from the basics of choosing a niche and building an audience, to the more advanced tactics of monetizing your content and scaling your income.

So if you're ready to take control of your financial future and explore the exciting world of making money online, let's dive into "The Ultimate Guide to Making Money Online" and get started!

Chapter 1: Finding Your Niche - Identifying Your Online Income Opportunities

In order to start making money online, the first step is to identify your niche. This means finding a specific area of interest or expertise that you can focus on in order to build your online presence and create valuable content.

One way to identify your niche is to start with what you already know. Consider your hobbies, interests, and any expertise you have developed through your career or education. Think about what you enjoy doing and what you're good at, and how you might be able to turn that into a viable online income stream.

Another approach is to conduct research into potential niches that are currently in demand. This could involve using keyword research tools to identify popular search terms and topics, or browsing online marketplaces to see what products or services are currently in demand.

Once you have identified your niche, it's important to conduct further research and analysis to ensure that it is a viable and profitable option. This might involve analyzing your competition, assessing the size of your potential audience, and identifying any gaps or unmet needs in the market that you can address.

In order to establish your online presence and build a following in your niche, you will also need to consider your branding and messaging. This might involve developing a strong brand identity, creating a website or social media presence, and crafting compelling content that resonates with your target audience.

Overall, finding your niche is a crucial step in making money online, as it sets the foundation for all of your future efforts. By identifying a viable and profitable niche, and building a strong online presence around it, you can establish yourself as an authority in your field and create a sustainable online income stream.

One important consideration when identifying your niche is to assess the level of competition in the market. If there are already many established players in your chosen niche, it may be difficult to break in and establish yourself. On the other hand, if there is no competition, this may be a red flag indicating that there is not enough demand for your chosen topic.

To get a better sense of the competition in your niche, you can use tools like Google Keyword Planner or SEMrush to analyze search volume and see what keywords your competitors are targeting. You can also browse online forums, social media groups, and other communities related to your niche to see who the major players are and what topics are currently popular.

Another important factor to consider when identifying your niche is the size and demographics of your potential audience. It's important to have a clear understanding of who your target audience is, what their needs and pain points are, and how you can create content that speaks directly to them.

You can use tools like Google Analytics, Facebook Audience Insights, and other market research tools to better understand your audience and their behaviors. This can help you to create more targeted and effective content, and to position yourself more effectively within your niche.

Ultimately, the key to identifying your niche is to find a topic that you are passionate about and that you have the expertise to speak on. By focusing on a niche that you are truly interested in, you will be more motivated to create valuable content and build a loyal following, which is essential for long-term success in making money online.

When selecting a niche, it's also important to consider the potential income streams that you can leverage within that niche. For example, if you are interested in the health and wellness space, you might consider creating and selling digital products like ebooks, online courses, or coaching services. Alternatively, you could generate income through affiliate marketing, sponsored content, or advertising.

It's also worth considering the long-term potential of your chosen niche. You want to choose a topic that will be sustainable over the long term, and that will allow you to continue to grow and scale your income stream over time. This means thinking about emerging trends, potential changes in the market, and other factors that could impact the demand for your content.

Another important consideration is to assess your own skills and abilities when choosing your niche. Consider the types of content that you enjoy creating, whether that's writing, photography, video, or something else entirely. By choosing a niche that aligns with your strengths and interests, you will be more motivated to create high-quality content and build a following.

Finally, it's worth considering the overall "fit" of your chosen niche within your larger life goals and aspirations. Making money online can be a challenging and time-consuming endeavor, and it's important to choose a niche that aligns with your larger goals and values. This might mean choosing a niche that aligns with your personal passions, or selecting a topic that allows you to work flexibly and on your own terms.

Chapter 2: Building Your Online Presence

One of the most important steps in making money online is building a strong online presence. Your online presence is your digital "home base", and it's where you'll be showcasing your skills, content, and brand to potential customers and followers. Here are some key steps to building a strong online presence:

1. **Choose a platform:** There are countless online platforms to choose from, including social media sites, blogs, online marketplaces, and more. Choose a platform that aligns with your niche and allows you to showcase your content and brand effectively.

2. **Develop your brand:** Your brand is your unique voice and identity in the online world. Develop a brand that resonates with your target audience, and create consistent branding elements like logos, colors, and fonts.

3. **Create valuable content:** The heart of any successful online presence is valuable content. Develop content that educates, inspires, or entertains your target audience, and ensure that your content aligns with your brand and niche.

4. **Engage with your audience:** Building a strong relationship with your audience is key to growing your online presence. Engage with your followers through comments, messaging, and other forms of interaction.

5. **Optimize for search engines:** Making sure that your content is optimized for search engines like Google can help more people discover your content. Use keywords and phrases that are relevant to your niche and audience, and optimize your content for readability and user experience.

6. **Leverage social media:** Social media can be a powerful tool for building your online presence and growing your audience. Use social media channels to share your content, engage with your followers, and promote your brand.

7. **Choose the right domain name:** If you're building a website or blog, choosing the right domain name can be key to building a strong online presence. Your domain name should be easy to remember, easy to spell, and ideally should reflect your brand and niche.

8. **Develop a content strategy:** Creating valuable content is important, but it's also important to have a plan for how you'll create and share that content. Develop a content strategy that includes topics, formats, and publishing schedules, and be consistent in your approach.

9. **Use multimedia:** Incorporating images, videos, and other multimedia elements into your content can help make it more engaging and shareable. Use these elements strategically to support your messaging and enhance the user experience.

10. **Collaborate with others:** Building your online presence isn't something you have to do alone. Collaborating with other bloggers, influencers, or brands can help you expand your reach and build your reputation. Look for opportunities to guest post, collaborate on content, or participate in joint promotions.

11. **Monitor your analytics:** As you build your online presence, it's important to track your progress and measure your results. Use analytics tools to track metrics like website traffic, social media engagement, and conversion rates, and use that data to make informed decisions about how to grow and monetize your online presence.

12. **Build an email list:** One of the most effective ways to build a relationship with your audience and monetize your online presence is by building an email list. Offer a lead magnet or freebie in exchange for email addresses, and then use email marketing to nurture your leads and promote your offerings.

13. **Monetize your website:** If you're building a website or blog, there are a variety of ways to monetize your content.

These include displaying ads, promoting affiliate products, selling your own digital or physical products, or offering premium content behind a paywall.

14. **Utilize online marketplaces:** Online marketplaces like Etsy, eBay, and Amazon can be a powerful way to monetize your skills and products. Consider selling digital or physical products in a niche that aligns with your brand and expertise.

15. **Offer services:** Another way to monetize your online presence is by offering services in your area of expertise. This could include consulting, coaching, writing, design, or other services that align with your skills and brand.

16. **Use paid advertising:** Paid advertising can be an effective way to drive traffic and conversions to your website or social media channels. Consider using platforms like Google Ads or Facebook Ads to promote your offerings and build your audience.

17. **Leverage SEO:** Search engine optimization (SEO) is a long-term strategy for increasing organic traffic to your website. By optimizing your content and website for search engines, you can improve your visibility and attract more potential customers.

By utilizing these strategies, you can create multiple income streams and diversify your online presence. By experimenting with different approaches and learning from your results, you can find the monetization strategies that work best for your niche and target audience.

By taking a strategic and intentional approach to building your online presence, you can create a platform that helps you achieve your income goals and connect with a passionate audience. With a strong brand, valuable content, and a commitment to engagement and collaboration, you'll be well on your way to building a successful online income stream.

By following these steps, you can build a strong online presence that will help you attract followers, customers, and income. As you grow your presence, you'll also gain insights into what types of content resonate with your audience and how you can best monetize your efforts.

Chapter 3: Creating Compelling Content: Strategies for Engaging Your Audience

When it comes to building an online presence, creating high-quality, engaging content is essential. In this chapter, we'll explore strategies for creating compelling content that resonates with your target audience and helps you achieve your income goals.

1. **Know your audience:** Before you start creating content, it's important to have a deep understanding of your target audience. Who are they? What are their pain points, challenges, and goals? What type of content do they prefer, and how do they consume it? By understanding your audience, you can create content that speaks directly to their needs and interests.

2. **Use storytelling:** Stories have the power to captivate and engage your audience. Incorporate storytelling into your content, whether it's through case studies, personal anecdotes, or examples that illustrate your point. By making your content relatable and emotionally resonant, you can keep your audience engaged and build a stronger connection.

3. **Be authentic:** Authenticity is key to building a strong brand and connecting with your audience. Be honest, transparent, and vulnerable in your content, and avoid using gimmicks or tricks to manipulate your audience. By being true to yourself and your brand, you'll build trust and loyalty over time.

4. **Offer value:** Your content should offer real value to your audience. Whether it's through providing educational resources, inspiring ideas, or entertainment, your content should help your audience solve a problem or achieve a goal. By offering value, you'll build a loyal following and attract new followers through word of mouth.

5. **Use visuals:** Visual content is highly engaging and can help you tell a story or convey a message in a more impactful way.

Incorporate images, videos, infographics, and other visual elements into your content to make it more memorable and shareable.

6. **Optimize for SEO:** Search engine optimization (SEO) is an important consideration when creating content. By optimizing your content for relevant keywords and using best practices for on-page optimization, you can improve your visibility and attract more traffic to your website.

7. **Test and iterate:** Creating compelling content is an ongoing process of experimentation and improvement. Test different types of content, headlines, and formats, and track your results using analytics. Use what you learn to continually improve your content and engagement with your audience.

8. **Tell a compelling story:** Storytelling can be a powerful tool for engaging your audience and building a strong connection. Use storytelling techniques to make your content more interesting and memorable. This could include using anecdotes, case studies, or personal experiences to illustrate your point.

9. **Use emotion:** Emotion is a powerful driver of engagement and can help your content resonate with your audience on a deeper level. Use emotional language, such as words that evoke joy, sadness, or inspiration, to help your audience connect with your content.

10. **Use humor:** Humor is a great way to make your content more enjoyable and memorable. Incorporate jokes, puns, or lighthearted humor into your content, but be sure to use it in a way that's appropriate for your audience and brand.

11. **Incorporate data and statistics:** Data and statistics can add credibility to your content and help you make a strong case for your ideas or recommendations. Use research, surveys, or other data sources to back up your points and add depth to your content.

12. **Keep it concise:** In today's fast-paced digital landscape, attention spans are shorter than ever. Keep your content concise and to the point, and avoid unnecessary fluff or repetition. Aim to provide value in a clear and concise manner that's easy to digest.

13. **Use a variety of content formats:** Experiment with different types of content formats, such as blog posts, videos, podcasts, or infographics. Different formats can help you reach different types of audience members and keep your content fresh and interesting.

14. **Engage with your audience:** Engaging with your audience is a key part of creating compelling content. Respond to comments, ask for feedback, and foster a sense of community around your content. By engaging with your audience, you can build a loyal following and gain valuable insights into what resonates with them.

15. **Focus on a niche:** In order to create truly compelling content, it's important to understand your audience and what they're looking for. By focusing on a specific niche or topic, you can create content that speaks directly to their needs and interests. This can help you build a more engaged and loyal following.

16. **Use strong headlines:** Your headline is the first thing your audience will see, so it's important to make it compelling and attention-grabbing. Use strong action words, numbers, and questions to entice your audience to click and read more.

17. **Provide value:** In order to create content that resonates with your audience, it's important to provide real value. This could include sharing your expertise, providing useful tips and tricks, or offering unique insights. When your audience feels that they're getting something of value from your content, they're more likely to keep coming back for more.

18. **Be authentic:** Authenticity is key when it comes to creating compelling content. Be yourself, and don't be afraid

to share your unique perspective and voice. This can help you build a deeper connection with your audience and establish trust and credibility.

19. **Optimize for search engines**: Search engine optimization (SEO) is important if you want your content to be discoverable online. Use keyword research and on-page optimization techniques to make sure your content is optimized for search engines and can be found by your target audience.

20. **Measure your results:** In order to improve your content and make it more compelling, it's important to track your results and measure your performance. Use analytics tools to monitor things like page views, engagement rates, and conversion rates, and use this data to make informed decisions about how to optimize your content for better results.

By following these strategies, you can create content that not only engages your audience, but also drives results and helps you achieve your income goals. Remember to keep experimenting, learning, and refining your approach over time, and stay focused on providing real value to your audience with every piece of content you create.

By using these strategies, you can create content that engages your audience and helps you achieve your income goals. Keep experimenting, learning, and refining your approach, and stay focused on providing value to your audience with every piece of content you create.

By following these strategies, you can create compelling content that resonates with your audience and helps you achieve your income goals. Whether you're creating blog posts, social media content, or video content, keep your audience's needs and interests at the forefront of your mind, and aim to provide real value with every piece of content you create.

Chapter 4 : Driving Traffic to Your Site: Effective SEO, Social Media, and Advertising Techniques

In today's digital age, having a website is not enough to attract visitors. You need to drive traffic to your site in order to be seen by potential customers, increase brand awareness, and generate leads. There are various techniques that can help drive traffic to your website, including effective Search Engine Optimization (SEO), Social Media Marketing, and Advertising Techniques. In this response, we will discuss each of these techniques in detail and how they can help to drive traffic to your site.

1.Effective SEO Techniques:

Search Engine Optimization (SEO) is the process of optimizing your website to rank higher in search engine results pages (SERPs) for relevant keywords. SEO is a long-term strategy that requires patience, consistency, and time. However, when done right, it can bring a significant amount of targeted traffic to your website.

The following are some effective SEO techniques that can help drive traffic to your website:

• Conducting Keyword Research: Research relevant keywords that your target audience is searching for and include them in your content, metadata, and website structure.

• Creating High-Quality Content: Creating engaging and high-quality content that provides value to your target audience. This can include blog posts, videos, infographics, and other types of media.

• Building Backlinks: Getting other websites to link to your website can help boost your website's authority and improve your search engine rankings.

• Optimizing Website Structure: Make sure your website is well-organized, easy to navigate, and has a clear hierarchy to help search engines crawl and index your site more efficiently.

Conducting Keyword Research: Keyword research is an important part of any SEO strategy. By researching relevant keywords that your target audience is searching for, you can create content that is optimized for those keywords. This can help your website rank higher in search engine results pages (SERPs) for those keywords, increasing the chances of driving traffic to your site.

Creating High-Quality Content: Creating high-quality content is key to attracting and retaining website visitors. Your content should be engaging, informative, and provide value to your target audience. When creating content, make sure to optimize it for SEO by including relevant keywords and metadata.

Building Backlinks: Backlinks are links from other websites that point to your website. Backlinks are important because they can improve your website's authority and help improve your search engine rankings. To build backlinks, consider reaching out to other websites in your industry and asking if they would be interested in linking to your site.

Optimizing Website Structure: Optimizing your website structure is an important part of SEO. Your website should be well-organized, easy to navigate, and have a clear hierarchy. This can help search engines crawl and index your site more efficiently, improving your search engine rankings.

Mobile Optimization: With the increasing use of mobile devices, it's important to ensure that your website is optimized for mobile. This means that your website should be responsive, load quickly on mobile devices, and be easy to navigate on smaller screens.

Local SEO: If your business has a physical location, local SEO can help drive traffic to your site. Local SEO involves optimizing your website for local keywords and creating local business listings on sites like Google My Business and Yelp.

Site Speed: Site speed is an important factor for both SEO and user experience. A slow-loading website can result in a high bounce rate, meaning that visitors are leaving your site without engaging with your content. To improve site speed, consider optimizing images, reducing the number of HTTP requests, and using a content delivery network (CDN).

2. Social Media Marketing:

Social media is a powerful tool for driving traffic to your website. With millions of users worldwide, it provides a large audience to promote your products and services. The following are some effective social media marketing techniques that can help drive traffic to your website:

- Consistency: Consistently post engaging and relevant content on your social media platforms to keep your followers interested and informed.
- Visual Content: Use visual content like images, videos, and infographics to make your posts more engaging and shareable.
- Hashtags: Use hashtags to make your content more discoverable by users searching for specific topics or keywords.
- Engage with Your Followers: Engage with your followers by responding to their comments and messages, and encourage them to visit your website.

Consistency: Consistency is key when it comes to social media marketing. By consistently posting engaging and relevant content, you can keep your followers interested and informed. Make sure to post on a regular basis and at the times when your target audience is most active on social media.

Visual Content: Visual content like images, videos, and infographics can help make your social media posts more engaging and shareable. When creating visual content, make sure to optimize it for each social media platform's specifications.

Hashtags: Hashtags can help make your social media content more discoverable by users searching for specific topics or keywords. When using hashtags, make sure to use relevant and targeted keywords that your target audience is likely to search for.

Engage with Your Followers: Engaging with your followers is an important part of social media marketing. By responding to their comments and messages, you can build a relationship with your followers and encourage them to visit your website. Make sure to also encourage your followers to share your content with their own followers.

Influencer Marketing: Influencer marketing involves partnering with social media influencers to promote your brand and products. By partnering with influencers who have a large following in your target audience, you can reach a wider audience and drive more traffic to your site.

Social Media Advertising: In addition to organic social media marketing, you can also use social media advertising to drive traffic to your site. Social media platforms like Facebook and Instagram offer a variety of ad formats that allow you to target specific audiences based on demographics, interests, and behaviors.

Community Building: Building a community around your brand can help increase engagement and drive more traffic to your site. By creating a Facebook group or hosting Twitter chats, you can encourage your followers to connect with each other and with your brand.

3. <u>Advertising Techniques:</u>

Paid advertising can help drive traffic to your website by reaching a broader audience and targeting specific demographics. The following are some effective advertising techniques that can help drive traffic to your website:

- Pay-Per-Click (PPC) Advertising: With PPC advertising, you pay to have your website appear at the top of search engine results pages (SERPs) for relevant keywords. You only pay when someone clicks on your ad.
- Display Advertising: Display advertising involves placing banner ads on websites or social media platforms to drive traffic to your website.
- Retargeting: Retargeting involves targeting users who have visited your website before with ads to bring them back to your site.

In conclusion, driving traffic to your website requires a combination of SEO, social media marketing, and advertising techniques. By implementing these strategies, you can attract targeted traffic to your site, increase brand awareness, and generate leads. However, it's important to note that driving traffic to your site is an ongoing process that requires consistent effort and optimization.

Pay-Per-Click (PPC) Advertising: With PPC advertising, you pay to have your website appear at the top of search engine results pages (SERPs) for relevant keywords. You only pay when someone clicks on your ad. To create a successful PPC campaign, make sure to choose relevant keywords, create compelling ad copy, and optimize your landing pages for conversions.

Display Advertising: Display advertising involves placing banner ads on websites or social media platforms to drive traffic to your website. When creating display ads, make sure to choose relevant websites and social media platforms where your target audience is likely to spend their time.

Retargeting: Retargeting involves targeting users who have visited your website before with ads to bring them back to your site. To set up a retargeting campaign, you will need to install a tracking pixel on your website and create a list of users who have visited your site. You can then target these users with ads on social media or other websites.

Overall, by using a combination of these techniques and consistently optimizing your website, you can drive targeted traffic to your site and improve your online presence.

Remarketing: Remarketing involves targeting users who have visited your site before with ads to bring them back to your site. This can be a highly effective way to drive traffic and increase conversions, as these users have already shown an interest in your brand or product.

Social Media Retargeting: In addition to retargeting users who have visited your site, you can also retarget users on social media platforms like Facebook and Instagram. By installing a tracking pixel on your site and creating a custom audience, you can target users with ads on social media who have shown an interest in your brand.

Native Advertising: Native advertising involves creating sponsored content that blends in with the surrounding content on a website or social media platform. This can be an effective way to drive traffic to your site, as the content is relevant and engaging for the user.

Overall, it's important to regularly review and optimize your SEO, social media, and advertising strategies to ensure that you're driving targeted traffic to your site and meeting your business goals. By testing and experimenting with different techniques, you can find the strategies that work best for your brand and audience.

Chapter 5 : Monetizing Your Site: How to Choose the Right Income Streams for You

Monetizing your website or blog can be a great way to turn your passion into a source of income. However, choosing the right income streams for your site can be a challenging process. Here are some tips for selecting the right income streams for your site:

1.Determine Your Audience and Niche:

Before selecting income streams for your site, it's important to understand your target audience and the niche you're in. By understanding your audience, you can determine what types of products or services they are interested in and what they are willing to pay for.

2.Consider Your Traffic:

Another factor to consider when selecting income streams is your site's traffic. If you have a large audience, you may be able to generate significant revenue from advertising or affiliate marketing. If you have a smaller audience, you may need to focus on products or services that have a higher profit margin, such as digital products or consulting services.

3.Research Income Streams:

There are many different income streams available for website owners, and it's important to research the options and determine what is the best fit for your site. Here are a few common income streams to consider:

- **Advertising:** Advertising is one of the most common ways to monetize a website. This can include display ads, sponsored content, or paid product reviews. To generate significant revenue from advertising, you will need to have a large amount of traffic and a high click-through rate.

- **Affiliate Marketing:** Affiliate marketing involves promoting products or services on your site and earning a commission for any sales generated through your unique affiliate link. This can be a great way to monetize your site, especially if you have a strong relationship with your audience and can recommend products that are a good fit for their needs.
- **Digital Products:** Digital products, such as ebooks, courses, and printables, can be a great way to monetize your site. Digital products have a high profit margin and can be sold at any time without the need for additional inventory or shipping.
- **Consulting Services:** If you have expertise in a particular area, you can offer consulting services to your audience. This can include one-on-one coaching, group coaching, or online courses.
- **Sponsored Posts:** Sponsored posts involve working with brands to create content that promotes their products or services. This can be a great way to earn income, but it's important to ensure that the content is relevant and valuable to your audience.

4. Experiment and Test:

Once you have selected your income streams, it's important to experiment and test to determine what works best for your site. This may involve adjusting your pricing, testing different ad formats, or trying out new products or services.

In summary, choosing the right income streams for your site involves understanding your audience and niche, researching income stream options, and experimenting to determine what works best for your site. By taking the time to select the right income streams, you can turn your passion into a profitable source of income.

5. Build an Email List:

Building an email list is a crucial step in monetizing your site, as it allows you to stay in touch with your audience and promote your products or services directly to them. Offer a lead magnet, such as a free ebook or course, in exchange for their email address.

6. Create Quality Content:

Creating quality content is important for attracting and retaining an audience, as well as for promoting your products and services. Make sure your content is well-researched, informative, and engaging.

7. Use Upsells and Cross-Sells:

When selling products or services, consider using upsells and cross-sells to increase your revenue. For example, you could offer a higher-priced version of your product or recommend related products to your customers.

8. Consider Subscriptions:

Subscription-based models, such as memberships or access to exclusive content, can be a great way to generate recurring revenue. This can be especially effective if you have a loyal following that is willing to pay for access to your content or services.

9. Partner with Other Websites:

Partnering with other websites or influencers in your niche can help you reach a wider audience and generate more revenue. Consider partnering with other websites to create joint promotions or advertising campaigns.

10.   <u>Stay Current with Trends:</u>

Staying current with trends is an important part of monetizing your website, as it helps you to stay ahead of the competition and offer products and services that are in high demand. Here are some tips for staying current with trends:

- **Follow Industry Leaders:**

One of the best ways to stay current with trends in your niche is to follow industry leaders and influencers. Follow their blogs, social media channels, and podcasts, and pay attention to the topics and products they are promoting.

- **Use Social Media:**

Social media platforms like Twitter, LinkedIn, and Instagram can be great sources of information about trends in your industry. Follow relevant hashtags and participate in online discussions to stay up-to-date on the latest news and developments.

- **Attend Industry Conferences:**

Attending industry conferences and events can be a great way to connect with other professionals in your niche and learn about the latest trends and technologies. Take advantage of networking opportunities and attend keynote speeches and panels to stay informed about the latest developments.

- **Use Keyword Research:**

Using keyword research tools, such as Google Keyword Planner or SEMrush, can help you identify trending topics and popular search terms in your niche. Use this data to create content that is optimized for search engines and appeals to your target audience.

- **Read Industry Publications:**

Reading industry publications, such as blogs, magazines, and newsletters, can help you stay up-to-date on the latest news and developments in your niche. Subscribe to relevant publications and set aside time each week to catch up on the latest articles and trends.

- **Experiment with New Technologies:**

Finally, don't be afraid to experiment with new technologies and platforms to stay ahead of the curve. For example, you might try using virtual reality, artificial intelligence, or chatbots to engage with your audience in innovative ways.

By staying current with trends in your niche, you can position yourself as an authority and offer products and services that are in high demand. Remember to stay open to new ideas and technologies, and be willing to adapt your strategies as needed to stay ahead of the competition.

11. Use Analytics:

Using analytics software, such as Google Analytics, can help you track your site's performance and identify areas for improvement. Use analytics to track your traffic, conversions, and revenue, and use this data to make informed decisions about your monetization strategies.

12. Focus on User Experience:

Providing a positive user experience is crucial for building a loyal audience and increasing revenue. Make sure your site is easy to navigate, fast-loading, and optimized for mobile devices.

13. <u>Build Your Brand:</u>

Building a strong brand can help you stand out in a crowded online marketplace and attract a loyal following. Use consistent branding across your site and social media channels, and focus on building a strong reputation as an authority in your niche.

14. <u>Consider Donations:</u>

If you provide valuable content or services for free, consider adding a donation button or asking for contributions to help support your site. While donations may not be a significant source of revenue, they can help cover some of your site's expenses and show your audience that you appreciate their support.

15. <u>Network and Collaborate:</u>

Networking and collaborating with other website owners and influencers in your niche can help you grow your audience and increase your revenue. Consider guest posting on other sites, participating in online forums or social media groups, and reaching out to other website owners to explore collaboration opportunities.

By following these tips and experimenting with different monetization strategies, you can find the right income streams for your site and build a successful online business. Remember to stay patient and persistent, and don't be afraid to try new things in order to find what works best for you and your audience.

Finally, it's important to stay current with trends in your niche and in the online world in general. This will allow you to stay ahead of the curve and offer products or services that are in high demand.

By following these tips, you can effectively monetize your website or blog and turn your passion into a profitable source of income. Remember, it takes time and effort to build a successful online business, but with persistence and the right strategies, you can achieve your goals.

Chapter 6 : Affiliate Marketing: Maximizing Earnings through Strategic Partnerships

Affiliate marketing is a popular way for website owners to earn revenue by promoting products or services through strategic partnerships. In affiliate marketing, the website owner (the "affiliate") earns a commission on any sales generated through their unique referral link. Here are some tips for maximizing earnings through strategic affiliate partnerships:

1. Choose the Right Products or Services:

When choosing products or services to promote, make sure they are relevant to your niche and appeal to your target audience. Look for products that have high customer satisfaction rates and competitive commission rates.

2. Build Relationships with Affiliate Partners:

Building relationships with your affiliate partners can help you to negotiate better commission rates, gain access to exclusive promotions, and receive personalized support. Take the time to introduce yourself, provide value, and stay in touch on a regular basis.

3. Provide High-Quality Content:

Providing high-quality content that showcases the benefits of the products or services you are promoting can help to increase conversions and build trust with your audience. Consider creating product reviews, comparison articles, or "how-to" guides that help your audience make informed purchasing decisions.

4. Optimize Your Landing Pages:

Optimizing your landing pages can help to increase conversions and maximize earnings. Make sure your landing pages are visually appealing, easy to navigate, and optimized for mobile devices. Consider including clear calls-to-action and social proof, such as customer reviews or testimonials.

5. Experiment with Promotions and Incentives:

Experimenting with promotions and incentives, such as exclusive discounts or free gifts, can help to increase conversions and drive more sales. Work with your affiliate partners to create custom promotions that are tailored to your audience's needs and preferences.

6. Track Your Performance:

Tracking your performance using analytics software can help you to identify areas for improvement and optimize your strategies for maximum earnings. Use tracking tools to monitor your traffic, conversions, and revenue, and use this data to make informed decisions about your affiliate marketing strategies.

By following these tips and building strategic partnerships with reputable affiliate programs, you can earn a steady stream of revenue from your website while providing value to your audience. Remember to stay patient and persistent, and don't be afraid to experiment with different strategies to find what works best for you and your audience.

7. Stay Transparent and Ethical:

Being transparent and ethical with your audience is essential for building trust and maintaining your reputation as an affiliate marketer. Disclose your affiliate relationships clearly and honestly, and only promote products or services that you genuinely believe in and have personally used or researched.

8. Stay Up-to-Date with Industry Trends:

Staying up-to-date with industry trends and news can help you identify new opportunities and stay ahead of the competition. Follow industry blogs, newsletters, and social media accounts to stay informed about the latest developments and emerging trends in your niche.

9. Optimize Your SEO:

Optimizing your website for search engines can help you attract more organic traffic and maximize your earnings. Use keyword research tools to identify high-volume search terms related to your niche, and incorporate these keywords into your content and landing pages.

10. Diversify Your Income Streams:

Diversifying your income streams can help you reduce your reliance on any one affiliate program or revenue source. Consider offering other types of products or services, such as digital products, courses, or coaching, or exploring other monetization strategies, such as display ads or sponsored content.

11. Focus on Your Audience's Needs:

Ultimately, the key to success in affiliate marketing is to focus on your audience's needs and preferences. Provide value, solve problems, and offer solutions that meet your audience's needs and align with their interests. This will help you build a loyal following and earn their trust and loyalty over time.

By implementing these strategies and staying committed to building strong partnerships and providing value to your audience, you can achieve long-term success as an affiliate marketer and maximize your earnings. Remember to stay patient, stay persistent, and stay open to learning and adapting your strategies as needed to stay ahead of the curve.

12. <u>Choose the Right Affiliate Networks:</u>

Choosing the right affiliate networks can help you find high-quality products or services to promote, connect with reputable advertisers, and gain access to valuable resources and tools. Look for networks that have a strong reputation, offer competitive commission rates, and provide personalized support.

13. <u>Leverage Social Media:</u>

Leveraging social media can help you reach a wider audience and increase your exposure. Use social media platforms such as Facebook, Instagram, and Twitter to promote your affiliate products, build relationships with your audience, and drive traffic to your website.

14. <u>Use Email Marketing:</u>

Using email marketing can help you stay connected with your audience, promote your affiliate products, and nurture relationships with your subscribers. Use email marketing tools to create personalized and targeted campaigns, and include clear calls-to-action and links to your landing pages.

15. <u>Test and Refine Your Strategies:</u>

Testing and refining your affiliate marketing strategies can help you identify what works and what doesn't, and make data-driven decisions about how to optimize your performance. Use A/B testing, split testing, and other tools to experiment with different strategies and measure your results.

16. <u>**Focus on Long-Term Success:**</u>

While it's important to earn revenue from your affiliate marketing efforts, it's also important to focus on long-term success and building a sustainable business. Focus on building a loyal following, providing value to your audience, and creating a strong brand that resonates with your target audience.

In summary, affiliate marketing can be a highly effective way to earn revenue from your website, but it requires dedication, effort, and strategic thinking. By building strong partnerships, providing value to your audience, and staying committed to continuous learning and improvement, you can achieve long-term success and maximize your earnings as an affiliate marketer.

Chapter 7: Launching Your Own Products: Tips and Tricks for Successful Digital Product Creation

Launching your own products can be a highly effective way to monetize your website and build a sustainable business. Here are some tips and tricks for successful digital product creation and launch:

1. Identify Your Niche and Audience:

Before you start creating your product, it's important to identify your niche and audience. Determine what problems your audience is trying to solve, what their needs and preferences are, and how your product can provide value and meet their needs.

2. Research Your Competition:

Researching your competition can help you identify gaps in the market, uncover new opportunities, and refine your product strategy. Look at what other products are available in your niche, how they are priced, what features and benefits they offer, and how you can differentiate your product from the competition.

3. Choose the Right Type of Product:

There are many different types of digital products you can create, including ebooks, courses, software, apps, membership sites, and more. Choose the type of product that aligns with your skills, expertise, and resources, and that provides the most value to your audience.

4. Create a Strong Value Proposition:

Creating a strong value proposition is essential for convincing your audience to purchase your product. Clearly communicate the benefits and value of your product, and explain why it is unique, valuable, and essential for solving your audience's problems.

5. Use the Right Tools and Resources:

Using the right tools and resources can help you create high-quality and professional-looking digital products that your audience will love. Consider using tools like Canva, Adobe Creative Suite, or WordPress to create and design your product, and consider hiring freelancers or contractors to assist with specific tasks as needed.

6. Price Your Product Appropriately:

Pricing your product appropriately is essential for maximizing your revenue and ensuring that your product is accessible to your audience. Consider your audience's budget and spending habits, as well as your own costs and profit margins, when setting your product's price.

7. Create a Strong Launch Plan:

Creating a strong launch plan can help you generate buzz and excitement around your product, drive traffic to your website, and maximize your sales. Consider using tactics like email marketing, social media, paid advertising, and influencer marketing to promote your launch and generate interest in your product.

8. Provide Ongoing Support and Updates:

Providing ongoing support and updates can help you build a loyal following and maintain customer satisfaction. Consider offering customer support via email, chat, or phone, and provide regular updates and improvements to your product to ensure that it remains relevant and valuable over time.

By following these tips and tricks, you can create and launch a successful digital product that meets the needs of your audience, provides value, and generates revenue for your business. Remember to stay committed, stay focused, and stay open to feedback and continuous improvement as you work towards achieving your goals.

9. Build an Audience Before Launch:

Building an audience before your launch can help you generate interest and excitement around your product, and increase your chances of success. Consider using tactics like content marketing, social media, email marketing, and webinars to build a following and create a community around your brand.

10. Use Feedback to Improve Your Product:

Using feedback from your audience can help you identify areas for improvement and refine your product strategy. Consider offering beta testing, surveys, or focus groups to gather feedback from your audience, and use this feedback to make changes and improvements to your product before launch.

11. Create a Sales Funnel:

Creating a sales funnel can help you guide your audience through the purchasing process and increase your conversion rates. Consider using tactics like lead magnets, tripwires, and upsells to encourage your audience to make a purchase, and use landing pages and email marketing to guide them through the funnel.

12. Measure Your Results:

Measuring your results can help you identify what's working and what's not, and make data-driven decisions about how to optimize your performance. Use analytics tools to track your website traffic, conversion rates, and revenue, and use this data to identify areas for improvement and refine your product strategy.

13. Continuously Improve Your Product:

Continuously improving your product can help you stay relevant, competitive, and successful over the long-term. Consider using customer feedback, industry trends, and market research to identify new opportunities and areas for improvement, and use this information to make updates and enhancements to your product over time.

In summary, creating and launching your own digital product can be a highly effective way to monetize your website and build a sustainable business. By following these tips and tricks, you can create a high-quality and valuable product that meets the needs of your audience, generates revenue, and provides long-term success.

14. Set Realistic Goals:

Setting realistic goals can help you stay focused and motivated, and track your progress over time. Consider setting goals for your product launch, revenue targets, and customer acquisition, and use these goals to guide your strategy and measure your success.

15. Leverage Social Proof:

Leveraging social proof can help you build credibility and trust with your audience, and increase your conversion rates. Consider using customer testimonials, case studies, and social media endorsements to showcase the value of your product and demonstrate its impact.

16. Create a Compelling Offer:

Creating a compelling offer can help you persuade your audience to take action and make a purchase. Consider using tactics like limited-time offers, bonuses, and discounts to incentivize your audience to buy, and use persuasive copy and visuals to showcase the value of your product.

17. <u>Invest in Marketing:</u>

Investing in marketing can help you reach a wider audience and generate more revenue from your product. Consider using tactics like paid advertising, influencer marketing, and content marketing to promote your product and build awareness, and use A/B testing to optimize your marketing strategy over time.

18. <u>Build Partnerships:</u>

Building partnerships with other businesses and brands can help you expand your reach and tap into new audiences. Consider forming partnerships with complementary businesses or influencers in your niche, and collaborate on joint promotions or content to reach a wider audience.

19. <u>Stay Up-to-Date with Industry Trends:</u>

Staying up-to-date with industry trends can help you identify new opportunities and stay ahead of the competition. Consider reading industry publications, attending conferences and events, and networking with other professionals in your niche to stay informed and up-to-date with the latest trends and innovations.

By following these additional tips and tricks, you can create a successful and profitable digital product that meets the needs of your audience, generates revenue, and provides long-term success.

Chapter 8: Diversifying Your Income: Additional Ways to Make Money Online

Diversifying your income is a smart way to build a sustainable and profitable online business. While launching your own products and affiliate marketing can be effective income streams, there are also many other ways to make money online. Here are some additional ways to diversify your income:

1. Sell Digital Downloads:

Selling digital downloads can be a simple and effective way to generate revenue. Consider creating and selling digital products like ebooks, templates, printables, or digital art, and use platforms like Etsy, Gumroad, or Payhip to sell your products.

2. Offer Consulting or Coaching Services:

Offering consulting or coaching services can be a lucrative way to monetize your expertise and help others achieve their goals. Consider offering one-on-one coaching or consulting services in your niche, and use platforms like Calendly or Zoom to schedule appointments and meetings.

3. Host Webinars or Online Courses:

Hosting webinars or online courses can be an effective way to teach and educate your audience, and generate revenue at the same time. Consider creating and selling online courses or hosting webinars on topics that your audience is interested in, and use platforms like Teachable or Kajabi to host and sell your courses.

4. Sell Physical Products:

Selling physical products can be a way to diversify your income and offer your audience additional value. Consider creating and selling physical products like merchandise, clothing, or accessories, and use platforms like Shopify or WooCommerce to sell your products online.

5. Offer Sponsored Content or Advertising:

Offering sponsored content or advertising can be a way to generate revenue from your website or social media channels. Consider working with brands or businesses in your niche to offer sponsored posts or advertising space on your website or social media channels.

6. Participate in Paid Surveys or Online Focus Groups:

Participating in paid surveys or online focus groups can be a simple way to make some extra money online. Consider signing up for websites like Swagbucks, Toluna, or UserTesting to participate in paid surveys or online focus groups.

7. Become a Virtual Assistant:

Becoming a virtual assistant can be a way to monetize your administrative or organizational skills. Consider offering virtual assistant services like email management, social media management, or bookkeeping, and use platforms like Upwork or Fiverr to find clients.

By diversifying your income and offering your audience multiple ways to engage with your brand, you can build a sustainable and profitable online business over the long-term. Consider exploring these additional ways to make money online, and experiment with different income streams to find the ones that work best for you and your audience.

8. Rent Out Your Property:

If you have extra space in your home, you can consider renting it out on platforms like Airbnb or Vrbo. Renting out your property can be a way to generate passive income and cover some of your housing expenses.

9. Provide Translation Services:

If you're bilingual or multilingual, you can consider offering translation services online. Many businesses require translation services to reach global audiences, so there is always a demand for skilled translators. You can find translation work on platforms like Gengo or Upwork.

10.   Participate in Affiliate Programs:

In addition to promoting other people's products as an affiliate, you can also become an affiliate for larger companies like Amazon or Target. By promoting their products to your audience, you can earn a commission for each sale made through your unique affiliate link.

11.   Create and Sell Digital Services:

If you have skills in digital marketing, design, or programming, you can create and sell digital services online. You can offer services like website design, copywriting, or social media management, and use platforms like Fiverr or Upwork to find clients.

12.   Create and Sell Stock Photos or Videos:

If you're a skilled photographer or videographer, you can create and sell stock photos or videos on platforms like Shutterstock or

Getty Images. Every time someone uses your photo or video, you earn a royalty fee.

13. Start a Podcast or YouTube Channel:

Starting a podcast or YouTube channel can be a way to build an audience and generate income through advertising or sponsorships. By creating valuable content and growing your audience, you can attract sponsors who are interested in reaching your audience.

14. Create and Sell Online Courses:

If you have expertise in a particular subject or skill, you can create and sell online courses. Platforms like Udemy or Skillshare allow you to create and sell courses on a variety of topics, from cooking to coding. You can earn revenue from course sales and create a passive income stream.

15. Offer Coaching or Consulting Services:

If you're an expert in a particular field, you can offer coaching or consulting services to clients online. You can use platforms like Clarity or Coach.me to find clients and offer services like business coaching, career counseling, or personal development coaching.

16. Sell Digital Products:

In addition to creating and selling online courses, you can also sell other digital products like e-books, templates, or software. You can use platforms like Gumroad or Sellfy to sell your digital products and earn revenue.

17. Become a Virtual Assistant:

If you have administrative or organizational skills, you can become a virtual assistant and help businesses or individuals with tasks like email management, scheduling, or social media management. You can find virtual assistant opportunities on platforms like Upwork or Freelancer.

18. Participate in Online Surveys:

While online surveys may not generate a significant amount of income, they can be a way to earn a little extra money in your spare time. You can participate in online surveys on platforms like Survey Junkie or Swagbucks and earn rewards or cash for your opinions.

19. Invest in Stocks or Cryptocurrencies:

Investing in stocks or cryptocurrencies can be a way to generate income over the long term. While there are risks involved, investing in these assets can provide potential for growth and income. You can use online platforms like Robinhood or Coinbase to invest in stocks or cryptocurrencies.

20. Sell Physical Products:

In addition to selling digital products, you can also sell physical products online. You can create and sell products like handmade crafts, clothing, or accessories on platforms like Etsy or Shopify. You can also use Amazon's FBA program to sell and ship physical products.

By exploring these additional ways to make money online, you can diversify your income streams and create a sustainable income that supports your long-term financial goals. It's important to choose income streams that align with your skills and interests, and experiment with different strategies to find what works best for you.

Chapter 9 : Scaling Your Business: Strategies for Growth and Expansion

Scaling your business refers to the process of expanding your business beyond its current size, whether that's by increasing revenue, adding new products or services, entering new markets, or expanding your team. Scaling can help you take your business to the next level and increase your profits, but it also requires careful planning and execution. Here are some strategies for scaling your business:

1. Create a Growth Plan:

Before you start scaling your business, it's important to create a growth plan. This should include your goals, the resources you need to achieve those goals, and the metrics you'll use to measure your progress. You should also identify potential challenges and risks, and create contingency plans to address them.

2. Focus on Your Core Competencies:

As you scale your business, it's important to focus on your core competencies. This means identifying the products or services that are most profitable and that you're best at delivering, and doubling down on those. Don't try to be everything to everyone - instead, focus on what you do best and do it better than anyone else.

3. Leverage Technology:

Technology can be a powerful tool for scaling your business. Consider using software and tools that automate repetitive tasks and free up your time to focus on growth. This might include customer relationship management (CRM) software, project management tools, or automation software for marketing and sales.

4. **Hire the Right Team:**

As you scale your business, you'll need to build a team that can help you achieve your goals. This means hiring the right people with the skills and experience you need to grow. Make sure you have a clear idea of the roles and responsibilities you need to fill, and use job postings and interviews to find candidates who are a good fit for your company culture and vision.

5. **Establish Strong Partnerships:**

Partnering with other businesses or organizations can be a great way to scale your business. Look for partners who complement your strengths and can help you reach new customers or markets. You might partner with a company that provides a related service or product, or with an organization that has a similar audience.

6. **Expand Your Marketing Efforts:**

To scale your business, you'll need to reach new customers and expand your audience. This means investing in marketing and advertising, and experimenting with new channels and tactics. Consider using social media, email marketing, content marketing, or paid advertising to reach new customers and grow your audience.

7. **Monitor Your Finances:**

As you scale your business, it's important to keep a close eye on your finances. This means tracking your revenue and expenses, and making sure you have enough cash flow to support your growth. You may need to secure additional funding, whether through loans, investors, or other sources, to support your growth.

Scaling your business can be a challenging and rewarding process. By creating a growth plan, focusing on your core competencies, leveraging technology, hiring the right team, establishing strong partnerships, expanding your marketing efforts, and monitoring your finances, you can set your business up for success and achieve your growth goals.

8. Invest in Training and Development:

As your business grows, you'll need to invest in the training and development of your team. This means providing them with the tools, resources, and training they need to continue delivering high-quality work and supporting your growth. This might include workshops, online courses, or coaching and mentoring.

9. Innovate and Experiment:

To stay ahead of the competition and continue growing, it's important to innovate and experiment. This means trying out new products or services, testing new marketing tactics, or experimenting with new business models. Make sure you have a process in place for testing new ideas, and use data to make informed decisions about what's working and what's not.

10.   Build a Strong Brand:

Finally, as you scale your business, it's important to build a strong brand that stands out in your industry. This means creating a clear brand identity, developing a unique value proposition, and building a loyal customer base. Make sure you're consistently communicating your brand message across all channels, and that you're delivering a high-quality experience to every customer.

In summary, scaling your business requires careful planning, execution, and continuous innovation. By creating a growth plan, focusing on your core competencies, leveraging technology, hiring the right team, establishing strong partnerships, expanding your marketing efforts, monitoring your finances, investing in training and development, experimenting and innovating, and building a strong brand, you can set your business up for long-term success and achieve your growth goals.

Chapter 10 : Best Practices and Common Pitfalls: Proven Tips for Long-Term Online Income Success

Generating online income is a popular goal for many people, and there are a variety of approaches one can take to achieve it. However, not all methods are equally effective or sustainable over the long term. To increase your chances of long-term success in generating online income, it is essential to follow certain best practices and avoid common pitfalls. In this article, we will discuss some proven tips for long-term online income success.

1. **Start with a Plan:** Before embarking on any online income-generating activities, it is essential to have a clear plan in place. This plan should include your goals, the strategies you will use to achieve those goals, and the specific actions you will take to implement those strategies. Having a plan helps you to focus your efforts and avoid wasting time and resources on activities that are unlikely to produce results.

2. **Choose Your Niche Wisely:** To generate sustainable online income, it is essential to choose a niche that is both profitable and aligned with your interests and expertise. A niche is a specific area of focus that you will target with your online income-generating activities. It is essential to choose a niche that is in high demand and has room for growth, but also one that you are passionate about and can speak to with authority.

3. **Build Your Platform:** To generate online income, you need a platform from which to do so. This may be a blog, a website, a YouTube channel, or a social media profile. Your platform should be optimized for the niche you have chosen and should provide value to your target audience. It is essential to focus on creating high-quality content that is engaging and informative, as this will help you to build an audience and establish yourself as an authority in your niche.

4. **Monetize Your Platform:** There are many ways to monetize an online platform, including advertising, affiliate marketing, sponsored content, and selling digital or physical products. To generate sustainable income, it is essential to choose monetization methods that align with your niche and provide value to your audience. It is also important to avoid over-reliance on any one monetization method, as this can make your income stream vulnerable to fluctuations in the market.

5. **Focus on Consistency:** Consistency is key to long-term success in generating online income. This means showing up regularly on your platform, creating high-quality content, and engaging with your audience. It is also essential to stay up-to-date with industry trends and adapt your strategies as needed to stay relevant and provide value to your audience.

6. **Build an Email List:** Building an email list is an effective way to communicate with your audience and keep them engaged with your content. By collecting email addresses, you can send newsletters, promotions, and other content directly to your subscribers' inboxes. This helps to build a relationship with your audience and increases the likelihood that they will make a purchase or take other desired actions.

7. **Diversify Your Income Streams:** Relying on a single income stream can be risky, as it makes your income vulnerable to fluctuations in the market. Diversifying your income streams by incorporating multiple monetization methods, such as advertising, affiliate marketing, and selling products, can help to create a more stable and sustainable income stream.

8. **Invest in Education and Training:** The online income landscape is constantly evolving, so it is essential to stay up-to-date with the latest trends and best practices. Investing in education and training, such as online courses, webinars, and coaching, can help you to stay ahead of the curve and make

more informed decisions about your online income-generating activities.

9. **Track Your Results:** Tracking your results is essential for understanding what is working and what is not in your online income-generating activities. By tracking metrics such as traffic, engagement, and conversion rates, you can make data-driven decisions about where to focus your efforts and how to optimize your strategies for maximum results.

10. **Focus on Long-Term Relationships:** Building long-term relationships with your audience is critical to sustained online income success. By providing value, engaging with your audience, and creating a sense of community, you can build a loyal following that will be more likely to make purchases and recommend your content to others.

Common Pitfalls to Avoid:

1. **Lack of Planning:** Starting an online income-generating activity without a clear plan in place is a common pitfall. Without a plan, it is easy to get distracted and waste time and resources on activities that are unlikely to produce results.

2. **Choosing the Wrong Niche:** Choosing a niche that is not aligned with your interests and expertise or one that is too competitive or not in demand can lead to frustration and lack of success.

3. **Focusing Too Much on Monetization:** Focusing too much on monetization can lead to a lack of focus on creating high-quality content and building an engaged audience. It is important to balance monetization with providing value to your audience.

4. **Lack of Consistency:** Inconsistency in creating content and engaging with your audience can lead to a lack of momentum and stunted growth.

5. **Overcommitting:** It's important to avoid overcommitting yourself to too many activities or strategies. Trying to do too

much can lead to burnout and reduce the effectiveness of your efforts.

6. **Ignoring Analytics:** Analytics provide valuable insights into how your online income-generating activities are performing. Ignoring or not properly utilizing analytics can lead to missed opportunities and an inability to optimize your strategies.

7. **Lack of Patience:** Generating sustainable online income takes time and effort. It's important to be patient and focus on long-term success, rather than expecting immediate results.

8. **Failure to Adapt:** The online income landscape is constantly evolving, and it's essential to stay adaptable and willing to make changes to your strategies as needed to stay ahead of the curve.

By following these best practices and avoiding common pitfalls, you can increase your chances of long-term success in generating online income. Remember to stay focused on providing value to your audience, building relationships, and adapting to changes in the market, and you can achieve your financial goals over the long term.

In conclusion, generating online income requires a combination of strategic planning, consistent effort, and a focus on providing value to your audience. By choosing your niche wisely, building a strong platform, and monetizing effectively, you can create a sustainable income stream that allows you to achieve your financial goals over the long term.

<u>Conclusion :</u>

In conclusion, making money online can be a viable option for those who are willing to put in the effort and time to learn and develop the necessary skills. It's important to approach online income-generating opportunities with a critical eye and do thorough research before investing time and resources into them.

Sure! Making money online has become increasingly popular in recent years, especially with the rise of the gig economy and the growth of the digital economy. There are a variety of ways to earn money online, including starting a blog, creating and selling digital products, providing online coaching or consulting services, and more.

One advantage of making money online is that it can offer flexibility and freedom. Many online business owners and freelancers are able to work from anywhere and set their own schedules. However, it's important to note that earning a sustainable income online often requires significant time and effort, especially when starting out.

Another important factor to consider when attempting to make money online is the potential risks and challenges. The internet is full of scams and frauds, so it's important to be cautious and do thorough research before investing time or money in any online venture.

Overall, making money online can be a viable option for those willing to put in the work and approach it with a realistic and strategic mindset. As with any other type of work or business, success often comes down to a combination of skill, dedication, and a bit of luck.

Sure, here are a few more points to consider when it comes to making money online:

1. It's important to choose a niche or area of expertise that you're passionate about or interested in. This can help you stay motivated and engaged in your work, which is essential when it comes to building a successful online business.
2. Building an online presence and reputation is important when it comes to earning money online. This may involve creating a website, social media profiles, and other online assets that showcase your skills and expertise.
3. It's important to be patient and persistent when building an online business or trying to earn money online. Success rarely happens overnight, and it often takes time and effort to build a sustainable income stream.
4. One of the benefits of making money online is that there are often lower barriers to entry than traditional businesses. You may not need a large amount of startup capital or specialized equipment, and you may be able to work from home or a remote location.
5. However, it's important to be aware that competition can be high in many online niches, and it may take some time and effort to stand out from the crowd. It's also important to have a solid understanding of digital marketing and search engine optimization, which can help drive traffic and sales to your online business.

In summary, making money online can offer a range of benefits, but it's important to approach it with a realistic and strategic mindset, as well as a willingness to put in the time and effort required to build a sustainable income stream.

Table des matières

Introduction 1

Chapter 1: Finding Your Niche - Identifying Your Online Income Opportunities 3

Chapter 2: Building Your Online Presence 6

Chapter 3: Creating Compelling Content: Strategies for Engaging Your Audience 10

Chapter 4 : Driving Traffic to Your Site: Effective SEO, Social Media, and Advertising Techniques 15

Chapter 5 : Monetizing Your Site: How to Choose the Right Income Streams for You 22

Chapter 6 : Affiliate Marketing: Maximizing Earnings through Strategic Partnerships 29

Chapter 7: Launching Your Own Products: Tips and Tricks for Successful Digital Product Creation 34

Chapter 8: Diversifying Your Income: Additional Ways to Make Money Online .. 39

Chapter 9 : Scaling Your Business: Strategies for Growth and Expansion 44

Chapter 10 : Best Practices and Common Pitfalls: Proven Tips for Long-Term Online Income Success 48

Conclusion 52